CONTEMPORARY WRITERS IN CHRISTIAN PERSPECTIVE
EDITED BY RODERICK JELLEMA

T. S. Eliot

A CRITICAL ESSAY
BY NEVILLE BRAYBROOKE

WILLIAM B. EERDMANS / PUBLISHER

To

Victoria, Brian and Emma

CONTENTS

ACKNOWLEDGMENTS

In the course of writing this essay, I should like to thank the following for their help: Mrs. Valerie Eliot, Mr. W. H. Auden, Mr. Calvin Bulthuis, Mr. Robert Giroux, Mr. Philip Mairet, Mr. Robert Sencourt, Mr. Robert Speaight, Miss Wendy Metcalf of *The Times Literary Supplement,* and the Staff of the British Museum Reading Room. I am deeply grateful to my wife for all her encouragement, and to Dr. Lucca Ega, Professor Fooff Ramu, and Mr. Robert Rubens for several valuable suggestions. Excerpts from T. S. Eliot's books are printed by permission of Harcourt, Brace, and World, and Farrar, Straus, and Giroux.

London
December, 1966   —N. B.

I. Introduction

IN DECEMBER, 1917, A MR. CHARLES AUGUSTUS CONYBEARE was led to ask an overwhelming question: *Where do authors get their ideas from?* He gave as his address the Carlton Club, Liverpool, and he insisted that he was used to documentation in such matters. Mr. Conybeare was none other than T. S. Eliot: it was one of those disguises in which the poet delighted to indulge; an early example of that gentle buffoonery that was to become so developed in later years. Many of the disguises became well-known — the Aged Eagle and Old Possum; but others were less so — Gus Krutzsch, the 1921 pseudonym that he used in *The Tyro,* or the Deliberate Pedant who, when invited by I. A. Richards to join him in the 'Twenties in Peking, replied: "I do not care to visit any country which has no native cheese."

This playing of a part — Eliot even toyed seriously with the idea of playing Becket in his film version of *Murder in the Cathedral* — often informed his lecture manner. One moment on the platform he would be defining the poet's role as an attempt "to express the greatest emotional intensity of his time, based on whatever his time happened to think," and another he would be summing up a poet's career as "a mug's game." In the last pamphlet that he published before his death in 1965, a study of George Herbert specially written for the British Council in 1962, he commented on the seventeenth century poet's "cunning use of the learned and the common word, to give the sudden shock of surprise and delight." He cited the instance: "My thoughts are all a case of knives." Similar tactics were a mark of his own style. In both his poetry and prose, expected platitudes are suddenly kicked into life by surprise endings: "I have measured out my life *with coffee spoons,"* or: "The end of understanding poetry is enjoyment, and . . . this enjoyment is *gusto* disciplined by taste" (my italics).

At the time when Eliot invented Mr. Conybeare, he was the assistant editor on *The Egoist,* being employed at a salary of £1 a week in the absence of Richard Aldington, who had been called up for military service. Critical comment was invited from readers at the end of 1917, and in order to get it going it fell to the assistant editor to invent five correspondents. Apart from Mr. Conybeare, these included the Reverend Charles James Grimble of Leays who thought it good to keep "minds open and liberal by contemplation of foreign ways"; Mr. J. A. D. Spence who wrote from Thridslington Grammar School to praise Edmund Gosse, and to deplore an Ezra Pound translation of Ovid; Miss Helen B. Trundlett of Batton, Kent, who saw the war as a "Great Ordeal which was proving the well-spring of a Renaissance of English poetry"; and Miss Muriel A. Schwarz of 60 Alexandra Gardens, Hampstead, who thought that an article by Wyndham Lewis had cast "a slur upon the cheery philosophy of the brave boys in the trenches."

All his life Eliot showed himself not only a master at making up names and surnames, but at investing them with a background and history. In his fifth and final play, *The Elder Statesman,* Gomez tells Lord Claverton:

> You've changed your name too, since I saw you.
> When we were up at Oxford, you were plain Dick Ferry.
> Then, when you married, you took up your wife's name
> And became Mr. Richard Claverton-Ferry;
> And finally, Lord Claverton . . . .

J. Alfred Prufrock, who was first presented to the public in the June issue of *Poetry Chicago* in 1911, is undoubtedly his most famous creation. Yet until his dying day, he never revealed what the J. stood for — though he did once let slip to a university audience that Prufrock was a young, not middle-aged, man. Eliot believed in allowing the poetry to talk for itself. He believed too that middle-age did not begin before 55.

Often the surnames of his characters contain puns. Geron in Greek means an old man, but Gerontion has a built-in qualification: it means a little old man. Or, in *The Confidential Clerk* there is Lucasta Angel who is said to be "rather flighty." Or, in the case of the Jellicle Cats, the name may be a play on "angelical." "Jellicle" derives from " 'gelical," and "jellico" from "angelica." Nor do I think it farfetched to point out such etymology, because if Eliot in 1920 could speak of "Christ the tiger," why, two decades later, might not the dance of the Jellicles offer "a clear image of heaven," and an invitation thither to join in the ball? For half a century Dante's poetry remained Eliot's "most persistent and deepest influence," and in both poets dancing is frequently related, both directly and indirectly, to paradisal themes.

> In daunsinge, signifying matrimonie —
> A dignified and commodious sacrament

are lines that occur in *East Coker*.

When reading "The Song of the Jellicles" aloud to children, I have often noticed a shock of surprise and delight go through them at the lines:

> Reserving their terpischorean powers
> To dance by the light of the Jellicle Moon.

Some long words do not have to be understood to create a sense of enjoyment in the listener — whatever his age. This invocation to Terpischore, the Greek Muse of dancing, is a case in point. Indeed, magical invocations such as this play a significant part in *Old Possum's Practical Book of Cats* and reveal, beneath the outward fooling, both a practical and serious intent. Whole considerations of wrongdoing and the need for tolerance can be disguised in "the prettie tales of wolves and sheepe," wrote Sir Philip Sydney. Likewise, it is only a literary ploy when Eliot dismisses as "Five Finger Exercises" his lines on a Persian cat, a Yorkshire terrier, and a duck in the park.

These exercises appeared originally in the January number of *The Criterion* of 1933, and what they really amount to are notes on the ground that the poet had covered up to then, and hints of some of the things yet to come. Only "every five or ten years" can inspiration be released in full flood, because in the years between there must be much practice, much learning "to sit still," and much patience. That is why in Eliot, after each reading, fresh meanings emerge: the process is at once both gradual and cumulative. For all the time there is at work in each poem, and in the poems as a whole, a contrapuntal movement in which the sacred and the profane, the matter-of-fact and the fanciful, make their own comment on each other.

Sometimes, too, a poet can become a medium through which the unnamed feelings that lie in the unconscious of those about him can be lifted from the level of personal autobiography to that of public statement; and when this happens, the power is given to the poet to signify the exultation, the boredom and the despair of a complete generation. Many may have undergone these unnamed feelings once or twice in their lives, but it is only the great writer who can put them into words "every five or ten years."

II. Biography

ELIOT FIRST BEGAN TO WRITE WHEN HE WAS 7 — THOUGH there was some confusion in his mind then as to how exactly he should sign his work. A two-page life of "George Washington" composed at this period ends with a characteristic touch and provides a foretaste of his distinctive use of repetition:

> And then he died, of course. He was never said to say a *lie*.
> He died at Mt. Vernon.

This one and only excursion of his into historical biography is signed on its title page — Thos. S. Eliot, S.A., Editor of *The Fireside*. Yet on the next page of the manuscript there appears the familiar T. S. Eliot signature. (Mrs. Valerie Eliot, the poet's widow, tells me that she thinks the S.A. stood for Smith Academy — the school founded by his grandfather and to which he was sent later.)

The Fireside is described on its cover, in the editor's own handwriting, as "a little paper containing Fiction, Gossip, Theatre. . . . " This early insistence on the term "little paper" is worth stressing, because Eliot never lost his interest in "little reviews" — whether as a contributor, editor, subscriber or patron. When printers' bills were pressing about my own *Wind and the Rain* quarterly of the 'Forties, and he had helped out, I remember him saying: "Such magazines have an influence far beyond their sales." When he had worked on *The Egoist* it had never acquired a subscription list of more than 185, and later when he launched his own quarterly, *The Criterion,* its subscription list never rose above 800. In the case of his first editorial venture, each issue of *The Fireside* consisted of one single copy written entirely by himself and intended solely for domestic circulation. The Eliots were a literary household.

In the 1670s Andrew Eliot, one of their ancestors, had left the village of East Coker in Somerset to cross the Atlantic and settle in Massachusetts. By the time that Thomas Stearns Eliot was born on September 26th, 1888, part of the family had been settled for several generations in St. Louis Missouri. Two comments by the poet about his home town — one direct and one indirect — illustrate well the impact that it made. "I feel," he wrote in a local newspaper in 1930, "that there is something in having passed one's childhood beside [a] big river [like the Mississippi] which is incommunicable to those who have not." Again, in the sixth verse of his poem "Burbank with a Baedeker; Bleistein with a Cigar," there is the phrase "money in furs" — a phrase that he probably often heard in his boyhood, since St. Louis had grown prosperous on the fur trade. "Home is where one starts from," writes the poet in the *Four Quartets*.

Many of his ancestors had been scholars, clergymen, and minor men of letters, and several Boston relatives featured in his early work — notably his maiden aunt Miss Helen Slingsby and his cousins. "Cousin Harriet, here is the *Boston Evening Transcript*," ends one poem.

His mother had English roots. Forty years before Andrew Eliot had left East Coker in the seventeenth century, her ancestors had also emigrated with the original settlers to Massachusetts; and like the Eliots, the Stearns family too had literary blood in its veins. Charlotte Chauncy Stearns was a poet and dramatist in her own right. Children born late in a woman's life are frequently gifted with genius, and when her seventh and most famous child arrived, she was already 45. Three decades later when he sent her *The Waste Land* to read, and she was well advanced into her seventies, she championed his innovations against the criticisms made by the older, more conservative elements of the family.

When Eliot himself was well advanced into the seventies, he began one essay: "The family background of a man of genius is always of interest," and then went on to argue that this interest was increased if the man in question thought his ancestry "important to his career." Eliot thought his own very important and repeatedly referred to it. At a paper read at the centenary celebration held for Washington University in 1953, before turning to his subject in hand, which was "American Literature and the American Language," Eliot began with some preliminary remarks about his boyhood. He talked of the St. Louis City tramcars whose terminus in Forest Park, on the outskirts, meant for him "as a child, the beginning of the Wild West"; he spoke of how the idea of a university for his family was epitomized by Washington University; and he told his listeners that the Unitarian Church of the Messiah (then situated in the same road as his home in Locust Street) had represented for "us . . . [my sisters and elder brother] the Church." City, University and Church became for them the three symbols of Community, Education and Religion. He summed up: "I am very well satisfied with having been born in St. Louis: in fact I think I was fortunate to have been born there, rather than in Boston, or New York, or London."

In his poetry there were to be constant returns to the long dark Mississippi River; to the ailanthus trees growing along its banks; to the flaming cardinal birds flying over it; and to the high limestone bluffs nearby in which he and other boys searched for fossilized shellfish. It was at this period that an Irish nurserymaid called Annie Dunne, to whom he was affectionately attached, first turned his attention to Catholicism. He remembered on one occasion being taken by her to "a little Catholic Church [in St. Louis]." Likewise, he told Kristin Smidt, a Norwegian critic of his work, that an engraving of Murillo's Immaculate Conception, which hung in his parents' bedroom, had made a lasting impression on his memory, an impression that could be traced in some of his later work, especially *Ash-Wednesday*.

His mother too had written about the same picture, and in her notebooks are to be found draft poems on many of the subjects to which he himself turned: the Visit of the Magi, the Presentation in the Temple, and the Forty Days of Lent. Perhaps some lines in his *Four Quartets* show a filial debt. In *Savanarola*, a long dramatic poem published by Charlotte Eliot in 1926 when she was 83, she gives these words to the condemned Dominican:

> This is the Hall that grew with my desire
> And quick winged words that flew like shafts of fire.

10

Part IV of *Little Gidding* ends:

> We only live, only suspire
> Consumed by either fire or fire.

Earlier I quoted from the second Quartet the lines about dancing and about matrimony being "a dignified and commodious sacrament." That is a simple derivation from Sir Thomas Elyot's reference to "the dignitie and commoditie" of marriage. Sir Thomas had been encouraged by Henry VIII in the compilation of a Latin-Greek lexicon, and his other works, such as the *Boke of the Governour* (from which the passage on matrimony comes) or his tract on St. Cyprian, show him to have been an author whose aim was to make use of the writings of antiquity for the instruction and edification of his contemporaries. But to a twentieth century poet, born an American and obsessed by the idea of aristocracy and royalty, here was a hereditary link to explore.

A review written for *The Harvard Advocate* in 1909 when Eliot was a graduate student and a member of the editorial board, underlines the obsession. The book had been Van Wyck Brooks's *The Wine of the Puritans,* and the reviewer quoted with enthusiasm the sentence: "I think a day will come when the names of Denver and Sioux City will have a traditional and antique dignity like Damascus and Perugia — and when it will not seem grotesque that they have."

Seven years later Eliot was to offer his own variation on this theme:

> J'erre toujours de-ci de-là
> A divers coups de tra là là
> De Damas jusqu'à Omaha.

But the variation was put cautiously in French. In those seven years he had spent one reading French literature and philosophy at the Sorbonne in Paris, then returned to Harvard to begin work on his thesis about *Knowledge and Experience in the Philosophy of F. H. Bradley* (published for the first time in 1964). There had followed a Sheldon Travelling Fellowship and a year at Merton College, Oxford. On leaving Merton — "Oxford is very pretty but I don't like to be dead" — he made a decision to stay in England, and in July, 1915, married. For two years he made his living as a schoolmaster — first at

11

High Wycombe Grammar School and next at Highgate Junior School where he taught "French, Latin, lower mathematics, drawing, swimming, geography, history and baseball." After this, he became a clerk in the Colonial and Foreign Department of Lloyds Bank in the City and remained there till 1925. "Eight very satisfactory years" was his verdict. During this period he lectured frequently, reviewed regularly, and wrote his memorable series of review articles on the Elizabethan and Jacobean dramatists. In 1927 he took out British nationality. No longer would an American's longing to link Damascus with Omaha in Nebraska be put cautiously in French. The ancestral Eliots of East Coker who lay in the village churchyard, and the Eliots who looked out at the Dry Salvages lying off the northeast of Cape Ann, would be invested alike with a shared "antique dignity." From now onwards, the family ties between the two worlds, the Old and the New, would be drawn tighter and tighter.

III. The Poems

ELIOT'S FIRST SLIM BOOK, *Prufrock & Other Observations,* WAS published in wartime England by the Egoist Press in the summer of 1917. It ran to 40 pages, had stiff buff paper-wrappers, and the edition was limited to 500 copies. It contained eleven poems and one prose piece called "Hysteria" (an experiment in prose rhythm). Most of the poems had been printed before, five of them having been included in Pound's *Catholic Anthology* of 1915.

The first and last poems are love songs — though love songs of a very different order from each other and of quite a different range from what the Georgian poets would have considered apt or fitting. Prufrock's love song, which opens the collection, is addressed in its first line to "you and I." In "La Figlia che Piange," with which the collection closes, a young suitor is shown talking to a girl who stands on some garden stairs. So much for the first stanza. In the second and third stanzas, the poet takes over as an observer, and I choose the word observer for the poet because Eliot himself chose to use the word "Observations" about the poems in this volume.

In lectures, Eliot on several occasions drew attention to the three voices of poetry: the voice of the poet talking to himself he called the first voice; the voice of the poet talking to listeners he called the second; and the voice of the poet speaking through another character — a narrator, observer or actor — he called the third. In "La Figlia che Piange" the voice of the young suitor and the poet-observer are brought momentarily together in the second stanza as "we." It is the one clue by which a careful listener can tell that the poem is made up of both objective *and* personal statement. Or, one way of looking at it might be to say that the suitor is the shadow of the observer, since what the poem really illustrates is the doubling of consciousness — a favorite Eliot device.

In 1964 Eliot referred to this particular poem as the most innocuous that he had written as a young man and consequently his most anthologized piece of the period. Certainly on its completion he wrote no more poetry for three years, concentrating his attention on metaphysics and philosophy, Sanskrit and Pali. Yet if the poem now seems innocuous enough, presenting no more than the end of an unhappy relationship with the understatement "I . . . lost a gesture and a pose," it does still serve as an early example (and at the time of publication what a pioneer example it must have been) of the way Eliot had adapted Henry James's belief that a place need not be made real only by description, but that it can be made just as real "by something happening there." Of course all that happens outwardly is that a man leaves a girl standing on the top of some garden stairs. Yet this brief leave-taking, and all that has led up to it, are so compressed — such is the poet's power — that long after the incident is over, or the book shut, its memory is still sufficient to amaze the "troubled midnight and the noon's repose" of the reader no less than the poet-observer.

J. Alfred Prufrock stands also on a staircase — perhaps the purgatorial stairway so loved by Dante from whose *Inferno* there is a passage quoted at the head of the poem. The love song of the title is a double irony, for Prufrock sings no song and gives no love. The "you and I" of the first line soon

13

becomes "I," and the "you" is not a woman. In fact when a woman is introduced into the poem, she is presented impersonally:

If one, settling a pillow or throwing off a shawl. . . .

Prufrock calls her "one" because he is frightened of any relationship that may involve him; he desexualizes her, so as to take away fear. For the crisis that the poem is concerned with is *Who am I?* — a crisis of self-identification that all Eliot's characters have to face sooner or later. "Do I dare/Disturb the universe?" asks Prufrock — though the irony is that even the question is not his own: it is a translation of a question to be found in a letter of Jules Laforgue's, dated 1881. The truth is that Prufrock has no personality to reflect. He is an echoing voice, lost in the social vacuum of Boston women talking of Michelangelo. His hell is a twentieth-century version of Dante's *Inferno*.

The poem was a dazzling one with which to begin a first book of poems. It had taken over a year to complete. The first lines had been written at Harvard, and he worked on the rest subsequently in France and Germany. The paring away, until all that remains is a timidity of tone, is masterly. And to test this, ask what, after 131 lines, really emerges about J. Alfred Prufrock and his supposed love life? Compare his monologue with Hamlet's "O what a rogue and peasant slave am I" — and how sharply the comparison will bring home the difference between a man of flesh and blood and his dilemmas of conscience, and a disembodied speaker whose references to Lazarus, John the Baptist, Hesiod or even Hamlet himself, do nothing to clothe the skeleton. For Prufrock is the voice of the skeleton in the cupboard crying "Know thyself" — and unable to communicate with himself or anyone. Moreover it is one of the paradoxes of the poem that the images ("the sky / Like a patient etherised upon a table") and the rhyming couplets ("afternoons" and "coffee spoons") leave a far more lasting impression than he does.

To some of their early poems, poets say: "Go away! Find a place for yourself in a book — and don't expect me to take any further interest." Just how far this poem had gone away was brought out in the 1950s when a critic asked the poet if he could remember the furniture wholesalers in St. Louis called Prufrock-Littau. He confessed that he could not, but added the saving clause that possibly the name could have lodged in his unconscious.

The relationship of the unconscious to the conscious was something that Eliot was to explore more fully in "Gerontion" — a poem that he had originally intended to print as a prologue to *The Waste Land,* but which, on Pound's good advice, he decided to include separately in *Ara Vos Prec* in 1920. This slim collection issued by the Ovid Press was limited to 264 copies. Several of the poems in it had been printed in the previous year by Leonard and Virginia Woolf at their Hogarth Press under the title of *Poems.*

"Gerontion," I believe, is one of the most difficult of the Eliot poems, and the one that has caused generally the greatest number of misreadings. It is important, at the outset, to realize that the whole monologue consists of an old man's "Thoughts . . . in a dry season." Nor is the old man the poet (Eliot would have been 32 at this time). Grover Smith, who has tracked down more of the poet's sources than any other living critic, makes the error of seeing Gerontion as the symbol "of a civilization gone rotten." The figures of Hakagawa, Mr. Silvero, Madame de Tornquist and Fräulein von Kulp who rise in the old man's thoughts are, he maintains, "the inheritors of desolation." On the contrary: these people are simply examples by which Gerontion chooses to express his sense of desolation, a desolation that he finds all around him — but rejects.

The difference between seeing Gerontion as a symbol, and Gerontion himself using people as symbols, is a subtle, but vital, one, if the poem is not to be falsely interpreted as a piece of Christian propaganda. For once the figures summoned by Gerontion are regarded as real people whom the old man has met, this then explains his comment that immediately follows his description of them: "I have no ghosts." At one remove, readers who happen to be Christians may find in the poem an illustration of spiritual drought — though all that Gerontion himself finds is his dislike of Christianity further increased by musing on the religious superstitions that have been practiced by so many believers whom he has known. Nor does his criticism stop short at Christianity: it applies to all forms of faith.

15

Parallel with this active dislike of religious faith goes a passive indifference to the powers of history and sex. Gerontion is speaking for a post-war Europe of disillusion when he says:

History has many cunning passages, contrived corridors

In 1919, this line might have suggested the passage of arms that was just over, and the creation of the Polish Corridor. Half a century later, it can still recall these things, but fresh interpretations can now be added: "contrived corridors" can mean to new readers the corridors of power at Washington or Whitehall. In other words, by using the third voice of poetry, Eliot was able to incorporate in the poem observations which, time has subsequently shown, can be made to stand for something larger than themselves. It was an effect that the poet had hoped for, because in the 'Thirties he had told the late F. O. Matthiessen that when a poet's examples are clearly rendered, the time will pass when they have any conscious reference to specific events and they will become instead "unconsciously general."

The last section of the poem turns to sex, but sex unsatisfied "when the sense has cooled"; and just as Gerontion no longer has any desire to change history — he accepts his impotence in the face of it — so the same impotence affects him physically. Even the springs of his emotion have dried up. In the final lines a gull battles vainly against the wind — and the wind was a symbol that Eliot often used for emptiness. The Shakespearean epigraph at the top of the poem speaks of after-dinner dreaming — though the irony is that Gerontion's monologue is really a nightmare, spoken at the moment of waking.

The poems that follow it in the 1920 volume offer "other observations" like the Prufrock volume — although most of them are made in the third, not first, person; and with this change from first to third person, goes a change from a deceptively confidential tone to more regular rhymed quatrains. In their mathematical precision and faultless syntax, there are many equations: in "Burbank with a Baedeker: Bleistein with a Cigar," Princess Volupine's three lovers are equated with Cleopatra's three lovers, and these poems, no less than the later five finger exercises, are examples of that striving toward

16

technical excellence by continuous effort which provides the necessary discipline for a poet to be ready to record the major moments of vision when they come.

Eight years passed between the writing of "The Love Song of J. Alfred Prufrock" and "Gerontion," and if the three books that appeared between 1917-20 suggest a prodigality of talent, it should be remembered that each volume was only a selection, not a collection, of what had been written. "All that the poet wishes to preserve" is a regular "blurb" writer's phrase. When Eliot became a publisher in 1926, he was to use it a great deal in regard to his own work, both prose and poetry.

The Waste Land was printed in the first number of *The Criterion* in 1922. It ran to 433 lines, and there were no "Notes" at the end about the sources on which the poet had drawn. They were simply added later to pad the whole thing out, because Liveright, the New York publishers, "wanted a longer volume and the Notes were the only available unpublished matter." Indeed, the "Notes" were really something of a literary spoof, for they add nothing to the poem as a poem — though they have provided commentators with an endless game of hunt-the-reference. Probably Pound best summed them up when he said: "As to the citations, I do not think it matters a damn which is from Day, which from Milton, Middleton or Augustine"; and probably Spender best put his finger on what attracted young poets to *The Waste Land,* when he declared that it was because "rhythmically the language was so exciting" (he himself was in his early teens at the time). For what contemporary then of Eliot's would dare to have made single lines of

Twit twit twit

or

Jug jug jug jug jug jug?

Their excitement too still communicates itself to the young.

In 1958 when I edited a symposium to celebrate Eliot's 70th birthday, I decided to give a section to the views of school children. One boy said he particularly liked the poem's foreign quotations from Latin, French, Italian, German and Greek: he enjoyed especially their unfamiliarity; thought they lent a professional touch to the whole thing; and saw them as sops to the best kind of human vanity because secretly every-

17

body likes to "pride [themselves] on [their] pronunciation of foreign words." Among the lines that he singled out was the last, based on the Sanskrit benediction with its triple repetition of the word

Shantih shantih shantih

which translated means "the peace that surpasseth understanding."

A girl, aged 14, spoke up for the inexplicable ecstacy of lines like

Weilala leia
Wallala leialala

She found expressed in them "all the pain in sound or joy produced since primitive creation." It may be worth putting on the record that the publishers, who originally commissioned the symposium, refused to issue it when I would not agree to cut out this section. So another firm took the book over — and two months after his birthday, Eliot wrote to me: ". . . the group of contributions by school children inspired me with awe and admiration. . . . "

E. M. Forster has described *The Waste Land* as "a personal comment on the universe," while Hugh Ross Williamson, one of the first critics to devote a whole book to Eliot, found in the poem "a cry from the wilderness, a call to repentance." These two verdicts by a liberal agnostic and a then Anglican priest, both made within a decade of the poem's publication, reflect two responses still shared by many. The response once so often trotted out in Left-Wing magazines of the 'Thirties, and then later incorporated in school textbooks — namely, that *The Waste Land* represented "the disillusionment of a generation" — was one that the poet firmly rejected. All he would concede was that for some readers the poem may have answered their wish-fulfillment to be involved in "the illusion of being disillusioned." Nor was he ever prepared to admit that an emotional landscape of desolation such as was called up by his use of "broken images," meant a separation from belief, since for him doubts and uncertainties represented varieties of belief. They raised questions — and to ask questions was a sign of life. That is why the generation after the second World War finds his poem as pertinent as their parents who

18

read it after the first. And if it is read by their grandchildren a quarter of a century from now, it will not be because of the historical situation which it mirrored in 1922, but because of the insight that it gives of a man's mind tormented by the problems and possibility of eternity.

To question is to think is to suffer. This is the Eliot method of approach here. In Tiresias he has chosen a narrator who has "foresuffered all"; and as the poet says, "the poem *is* what he sees." So choosing as a prophet an "old man with wrinkled female breasts," the poet is able, on a world level, to telescope history's Punic War between the Carthaginians and the Romans with the first World War, and to bring together, on a personal level, memories of drinking coffee in the Hofgarten with speculations on the Austro-Hungarian Empire. These, and a thousand other things, pass through the poet's mind in the opening 70 lines.

Contrast has always been one of Eliot's mainstays, and by adapting for his first line Chaucer's

> Aprille with his shoures sot (sweet)

to his own

> April is the cruellest month,

he has set against the medieval poet's spring picture of Cupid's darts and Canterbury pilgrimage, his own bleak landscape of dull roots and travel in a Europe of "unreal cities" just freed from the memories of war:

> Jerusalem Athens Alexandria
> Vienna London.

If memory and desire mix, it is to stir a sluggish sexuality:

> Exploring hands encounter no defence.

The comparison in Part III between the carbuncular house-agent's arrival at the typist's bed-sittingroom and Queen Elizabeth and Leicester riding downstream on the Thames in the royal state barge, could not be more pronounced. The April of Eliot is not a time of burgeoning, and what copulation there is, is mechanical, bored, and tired.

The Europe that Eliot sees through Tiresias's eyes is a world collapsing by trying to subsist on a civilized but non-Christian mentality. It would be a mistake however to accept this stric-

19

ture in too **narrow** or orthodox a sense. Eliot told Gabriela Mistral, the South American poet and Nobel Prize winner, that at the time when he was writing *The Waste Land,* he had seriously been thinking about becoming a Buddhist, and what the poem reflects is not only his interest in belief but his attempt to link up various beliefs whether their expression be Greek, Oriental, Hebraic or Christian. Ecumenical is not a word that has so far been applied to *The Waste Land,* but with the new winds of religious change blowing through the world, it is a word that may well sum up the spirit behind the poem as it comes to be read by new generations during the second half of the twentieth century.

In Eliot's next poem *The Hollow Men,* "the waste land" becomes "the dead land." Earlier drafts and sections had appeared during 1924-25 in *The Chapbook, Commerce, The Criterion* and *The Dial.* The final version however came out in *Poems 1909-25,* a volume issued by Faber & Gwyer (later Faber & Faber) — the firm that he was to join in the following year and to work with as a director for the rest of his life.

In his own words, *"The Hollow Men* [marked] a point of spiritual aridity in my career." He was 36. The monologue begun in "Gerontion," and continued by Tiresias, was now further developed — though this time with the help of a chorus of "stuffed men . . . filled with straw." In the five parts of the poem, consequence is nowhere related to sequence, and yet the movements flow together as smoothly as in a dream. The last line, on waking, comes as no surprise:

> *This is the way the world ends*
> *Not with a bang but a whimper.*

The poem begins with two different kinds of bang, both in the form of an epigraph. The first is "Mistah Kurtz — he dead," a dramatic last line borrowed from Conrad's *Heart of Darkness,* and the other is "A penny for the Old Guy," a traditional cry repeated all over England on November the Fifth.

Conrad in his novel writes: "All Europe contributed to [Mistah Kurtz's] making . . . His mother was half-English, his father half-French. . . . " His words were "common everyday ones . . . [though] they had behind them . . . the terrific suggestiveness of words heard in dreams." The poem explores the dream language between sleeping and waking, with infinite attention paid to sound, and with infinite variation brought to bear on the repetition of the words "death" and "kingdom": "death's dream kingdom"; "death's kingdom"; "lost kingdoms"; "death's other kingdom"; "death's twilight kingdom"; and Kingdom Come — *"For Thine is the Kingdom."* These thematic fragments, so to speak, emphasize the musical structure of the poem — and in 1951 Denis Aplvor, the Welsh composer, skillfully orchestrated the sequence for a baritone and male chorus. Incidentally, half in jest but half seriously, Eliot once described himself to Bonamy Dobrée as "a bellowing baritone."

Just as *The Waste Land* brings together a "mixing of memory and desire," so this poetic sequence brings together a mixing of dream and reality. "Death's dream kingdom" represents the death-in-life attitude that Tiresias saw all about him — an attitude which takes the meaning out of living and so signifies death, as opposed to death's other Kingdom, which restores meaning to life by positing a Kingdom Come. Yet though the poem develops these themes from *The Waste Land,* it does also in its closing section give some hint of that message of redemption which was to break through five years later in *Ash-Wednesday.* The hint is dropped by allowing fragments from the Lord's Prayer to interrupt a nursery rhyme which has been distorted from "Here we go round the mulberry bush" to *"Here we go round the prickly pear."* The poet has blended together, with complete success, the components of jazz rhythm and liturgical chant.

Undoubtedly, in a spiritual sense, this is Eliot's most revealing poem. But it also has something to add as straightforward autobiography. Ever since he was a child in St. Louis, he had loved the firework displays held on July the Fourth to celebrate the birth of his native Republic. F. V. Morley, one of his fellow directors, has recalled how on one July the Fourth they filled a large brass coal scuttle with "giant firecrackers" in the Boardroom of Faber & Faber. The morning was spent fixing up pulleys, so that at the given moment in the afternoon's meeting it would be possible to pull the scuttle under the Chairman and there let it explode, breathing fire like the best of dragons. Morley thinks it the most successful joint practical joke they ever played.

On November the Fifth, 1605, Guy Fawkes was discovered beneath the Houses of Parliament with several barrels of gunpowder; he was preparing to blow up James I and the government. The event is celebrated annually in England with firework displays. Faber & Faber have printed several books about the "gunpowder plot," including one by Hugh Ross Williamson.

When Eliot wrote *The Hollow Men* he had lived over ten years in England and was becoming accustomed to the English idea that change is seldom effected dramatically by blowing up a king and parliament. For instance, during Eliot's long residence in London — he was a townsman by nature — it would be difficult to say at what exact moment public opinion turned against capital punishment (he was against it from the start, although officially it was not abolished until he was over 70). Likewise, the Catholic religion that Fawkes had planned to restore by gunpowder slipped back three centuries later almost unnoticed. Such imperceptible changes that occur historically in England were something that he attempted to achieve poetically in his poetry. And *Poems 1909-25* was to be the last book that he published as an American, because within three years of its appearance he had decided to become a British subject. He had also declared himself a classicist in literature, a royalist in politics and an Anglo-Catholic in religion. The first two terms he was to qualify considerably in old age.

Ash-Wednesday is dedicated "To My Wife." In 1915 Eliot had married Vivienne Haigh-Wood, who to supplement their income in the early days of their marriage had given private lessons in French and German. Friends have recalled her as a gay chatterbox who wanted to enjoy life; who found her husband somewhat inhibited and inhibiting; and who yet worshipped him with all her heart. But she was frail, and suffered from feeble health which exasperated an already nervous temperament. Finally she succumbed to a hysterical psychosis and died in a mental hospital in 1947. Husband and wife had been separated for many years. A comment by Herbert Read, a frequent visitor to their home in the early days, says all that needs to be said of this domestic tragedy: "Posterity will probably judge Vivienne harshly, but I remember her in moments when she was sweet and vivacious; later her hysteria became embarrassing."

The first three parts of *Ash-Wednesday* were issued originally in French, American and English magazines, in that order, between 1928-29. His "blurb" for the book itself (of which he was both poet *and* publisher) is a classic of understatement. It reads: "[Here is] a new sequence of six poems with certain recurrent themes. They are further developments of a style used by the author in at least one of his *Ariel Poems."*

Eliot wrote five *Ariel Poems* in all: three in the 'Twenties — "Journey of the Magi," "A Song for Simeon," and "Animula"; one in the 'Thirties — "Marina"; and one in the 'Fifties — "The Cultivation of Christmas Trees." Part II of *Ash-Wednesday,* first printed under the title of "Salutation" in *The Saturday Review of Literature,* was intended to be another *Ariel Poem;* one that would complement his "Journey of the Magi," which had come out in August, 1927, and was intended by the publishers to be sold as a greeting card for Christmas. Five thousand copies were printed but unfortunately sales were poor, and ten years later the remainder were re-issued in mauve paper envelopes. (Copies once costing a shilling, were fetching up to three guineas in the 1966 second-hand book market in London.)

The Magus who recounts the journey in the poem assumes something of the air of a correspondent in *The Times.* "Satisfactory" is his comment on the place chosen for the mother's delivery, while the birth itself he remembers as a "Hard and bitter agony . . . like Death, our death." And his report ends with the short teasing statement:

I should be glad of another death.

Ash-Wednesday begins and maintains a far more personal style of approach.

Because I do not hope to turn again

it opens, and then passes on, as is fitting to its Lenten mood, to ask

For what is done . . .
May the judgement not be too heavy. . . .

Eliot uses the word "turn" as a pivot to allow him full scope to explore, turning upward and downward, all the twists on the spiritual stairway concerning the nature of grace, prayer, thought, action and observance. The temptations awaiting the religiously proud in *The Dry Salvages* where

> the way up is the way down, the way forward is the way back

are already anticipated in this earlier sequence.

In *The Waste Land,* Eliot had already shored against his ruins certain nursery rhymes and "fragments" from Dante, Gerard de Nerval and Ovid, and it was after writing this poem that Eliot admitted that he always began a poem first "with a rhythm." In *Ash-Wednesday* liturgical rhythm plays a significant part — in particular in Part II, which not only set the sequence going, but in which 23 lines out of 54 were devoted to a litany of praise divided between the Mother of God (whose Murillo image from Locust Street he never forgot), and a Beatrice-like figure who symbolizes the Church for him, just as Beatrice had symbolized Theology for Dante.

Between the first publication of this part of *Ash-Wednesday* in a magazine, and its final appearance in book-form, this litany underwent several changes. Changes for Eliot usually meant cuts — cuts that brought about a greater intensity in what was left. One of these cuts in the litany is especially revealing, and concerns the lines

> The single Rose
> Is now the Garden
> Where all loves end

which had formerly read:

> The single Rose
> With worm-eaten petals
> Is now the Garden
> Where all loves end

Presumably this earlier version was intended to refer to failings in the Church Militant — faults in her members, or even corruption in her ministry. It would be something that an Anglican of a year's standing would be far more likely to notice than a born Anglican. But by cutting the line, and so saving a reader the distraction of bothering about the Church's failings on earth, the poet was able in his revised version to link his vision with Dante's when, in the Church Triumphant, the poet of the

Paradiso sings of the saints as making up the petals of "a single snow-white rose."

The fact that the six *Ash-Wednesday* poems were not written in the order that they were composed brings home an important point about the fragmentary nature of religious experience. When faith is experienced — whether dramatically on the way to Damascus, in the damp savannas, or in boredom in the Edgware Road — there follow after the shining moment of receiving it, and before its final intellectual assimilation, many years of piecing together all the doctrines and dogmas that are involved. Such, too, is man's nature and its limitations, that the process can never be more than fragmentary.

Ash-Wednesday was written three years after the moment of faith struck, and on the last page the poet makes the "holy mother," and Beatrice "her blessed sister," the ground of his beseeching not only for himself, but for all men:

> Teach us to care and not to care
> Teach us to sit still.

Then for his last line, the poet joins his voice to the Church's refrain, changing "our" to "my":

> And let my cry come unto Thee.

Twelve years were to pass before that cry went up again in the greatest poem of his career and the greatest poem of the first half of the century — the *Four Quartets*. The years between were to be spent experimenting with plays, pageants and Aristophanic melodrama; translating St. John Perse, and editing *The Criterion* (it died in 1939); writing prefaces to contemporary poets like Marianne Moore and Harry Crossby, or past ones like Abraham Cowley and Tennyson, or to new novels like Djuna Barnes's *Nightwood* and past ones like Phillippe's *Bubu of Montparnasse* (both, as it happens, first novels). He contributed articles on John Donne, "Religion and Literature" and "Literature and the Modern World" to symposiums edited by Theodore Spencer, V. A. Demant and Allen Tate. Cat poems were tried out on children whom he knew, and sets of light verse in French, German and English (including an "Ode to a Roman Coot") were circulated privately among friends. Essays ancient and modern appeared on Ford, the Devotional Poets of the Seventeenth Century, the

Pensées of Pascal, and Wyndham Lewis, and book reviews ancient and modern on St. John of the Cross, Mrs. Gaskell, Humanism, and Middleton Murry. Starts were made on poems, and some five finger exercises published. The 1931 *Coriolan* sequence of four poems got half-way — then stopped. The decade was spent caring and not caring, waiting for that releasing rhythm — not the rhythm of Prufrock's voice, nor that of Gerontion or Tiresias — but the voice that would speak in the first person and yet be divested of all egoism — the "I" that would speak at the right moment the right words and, because the right words at the right moment, would come from

> A condition of complete simplicity
> (Costing not less than everything)

Burnt Norton was included at the end of Eliot's *Collected Poems 1909-35*. The poem is set in June, and it was during the summer of 1934 that he had chanced to visit this uninhabited Cotswold manor with its formal garden, low box-borders, and drained pool. When he had wandered in, he knew nothing of its past. Only later did he discover that another house had stood on the same site but been burnt down two centuries before. The effect of this casual visit, and this later knowledge, was an experience that he originally intended working into *Murder in the Cathedral*: but these passages added nothing to the dramatic action and so "had to be cut from the play." They became instead the beginning of a new poem. Further, in 1934 he had no idea that these left-over fragments were to form anything more than one poem, because it was not until five years later when he had completed *East Coker* that he conceived the thought of four quartets in which *Burnt Norton* would have first place, *East Coker* second.

East Coker is set in late summer. *The Dry Salvages,* which followed, is set in autumn, and January is the month of *Little Gidding* — that short, snap period in the English weather that so often brings with it a midwinter spring

> Suspended in time, between pole and tropic.

Listen to the poet catch its transitory hour when the hedgerow is blanched with the blossom of snow — a bloom "neither budding nor fading" and "more sudden / Than that of summer." Listen to him bring into being spheres and seasons of existence totally opposed to one another, and then, as in a dream, reconcile not only pole and tropic, spring and winter, but frost and fire:

> When the short day is brightest, with frost and fire,
> The brief sun flames the ice, on pond and ditches,
> In windless cold that is the heart's heat,
> Reflecting in a watery mirror
> A glare that is blindness in the early afternoon.

The last three Quartets were all first issued in *The New English Weekly,* "a review of Public Affairs, Literature and the Arts" that A. R. Orage had founded in 1932 and whose editorial committee from 1935 onwards included Eliot. Next, Faber & Faber brought out all three, as well as a reprint of *Burnt Norton,* in paper-wrappers at a shilling each. Finally in 1943 in America, and in England in 1944, his *Four Quartets* came out as one volume. Before the war was over, several commentaries had appeared. Since then there has been a spate of them, several of them far longer than the Quartets themselves, and some by people who, as the poet slyly remarked, "think they are writing about my poetry, [when they] are really writing about the kind of poetry they would have wished to write."

It is however generally agreed that the main themes of the Quartets are the pattern of history ("History may be servitude, / History may be freedom"; "History is now and England"); the relationship of time to eternity and its redemption ("Only through time time is conquered"); and the ties of ancestry ("In my beginning is my end"; "In my end is my beginning"). It is also generally agreed that as Beethoven, in his later work, "strove to get beyond music" (as Eliot once suggested), so in his *Four Quartets* the poet attempted something similar — namely, to achieve a poetry so transparent that in concentrating on it attention would fall not so much on the words, but on what the words pointed to. And in his rigorous stripping away of the poetic, such a pure poetry (as Paul Valéry too aimed for) is sustained.

Each Quartet is concerned with one of the four elements. In *Burnt Norton,* "vibrant air" fills the scene; in *East Coker,* "Earth feet, loam feet" echo from the past; in *The Dry Salvages,* "The menace and caress of wave that breaks on water" catches the ear; and in *Little Gidding,* "fire" and "pentecostal fire"

27

rage, burn and cleanse. All the passages I have singled out come from the first movements — though the linking of each particular Quartet with air, earth, water or fire should not be pursued too far, because each Quartet shares all the elements, and each element, when seen in the unfolding of the sequence as a whole, becomes more and more linked by cross-references. Due to these cross-references many of the lines acquire a multiple meaning. For example, within two different movements of one Quartet, the dove is used to symbolize both death and love: in the first, with its "flickering tongue," it has just let drop its basket of incendiary bombs on London, and in the second, with "flame of incandescent terror," it has just let drop its pentecostal blessing on those below. Or, there are the paradoxes: "the unseen eyebeam," or "the unheard music."

The second movement of *Little Gidding* is imaginatively the most intriguing, and the one that has puzzled critics the most. Several have thought that the ghost whom the poet meets and talks with in the blitzed London thoroughfare is Dante. He may be — but only partly so, because he is as well both "one and many." Partly he may be a composite figure made up of Dante's characters — Brunetto Latini from the *Inferno,* whose scorched features are here recalled as "brown baked features"; Arnaut Daniel, the Provençal troubador from the *Purgatorio,* who circles the fire which purifies the lustful, and whose memory was also summoned in *The Waste Land;* and Oderisi, the Gubbio painter from the *Purgatorio,* who shares a kindred melancholy with the Eliot ghost — "Last season's fruit is eaten." Other possibilities come from nearer centuries — Milton, whose shade haunts the next movement; Samuel Johnson, whose thoughts at 40 about oncoming age resemble those of Eliot at 54; and Mallarmé whose "*Donner un sens plus pur aux de la tribu*" is here translated as "To purify the dialect of the tribe." Another poet perhaps whose brown baked features fit the picture is Browning, who left his body on "a distant shore" and died in Venice in 1889.

This last speculation may seem a teasing one — but then Eliot loved to tease his public with puns and cryptograms. The enormous research industry set going by the "Notes" to *The Waste Land* was something in which he delighted. Even when he was 16, an adventure story of his about a whaling ship called the "Parallel Opipedon" is not without its leg-pull, since this name when split down into syllables becomes "O pipe do(w)n" — an early example of that tongue-in-the-cheek manner which so often lies half-hidden in his pages, but which no one who heard him lecture, or give readings, could miss. On one occasion he admitted himself foxed by the fifth stanza of *To a Skylark*. "There may be some clues for persons more learned than I," he said, "but Shelley should have provided Notes."

Two clues that he did drop concern the Quartets: one was that the compound ghost could "more or less" be partly identified with Yeats, and the other was that he had paid "particular attention" when composing his own Quartets to Bartok's Quartets, nos. 2-6. The recipients of these asides were Horace Gregory and J. C. Hodgart. Here too is the place to salvage a revealing sentence from the late Desmond McCarthy's *Sunday Times* review of *Little Gidding* — the first to appear. "The compound ghost," he asserts, "is both [the poet] himself and yet his mentor." Perhaps this best of all explains Eliot's encounter with the figure in the street who, throughout their conversation, remains both "intimate and unidentifiable."

In the third movement of *Little Gidding* more ghosts appear. They include a King, a statesman, an Archbishop and a Puritan poet. They can be identified as Charles I, the Earl of Strafford, William Laud, and John Milton. The last "died blind and quiet," but the other three went to the scaffold; moreover they were all royalists, whereas Milton was a republican. Taken as a quartet, within this particular Quartet, their views differ considerably — at some places irreconcilably — and it is only through time's perspective that the points can be seen where their lives transect and bisect.

The King was fond of Nicholas Ferrar's home in Little Gidding, Huntingdonshire, and held the place in "highe affectione." Laud had ordained Nicholas a deacon in 1625 — and twenty years later both died in the same year, one at home, one at the executioner's block. In the same year too, legend has it that the King after his defeat by the Scots at Naseby sheltered for the night at Little Gidding. The Ferrars, consisting of Nicholas and his family, his brother's family and his brother-in-law's family, had built a community whose life was ordered to a rhythm of religious devotion and good works; their name was held in esteem throughout the breadth of the land. Yet within two years of their founder's death, the community was scattered by Cromwell's Roundheads. Nor has Nicholas's experiment, of a religious community founded on the Christian family, ever been attempted again in the Anglican Church, just as Laud's hope for a united, loyal national Church in England with one liturgy has never come to pass. Both seem "lost causes" — like Milton's republicanism. Yet "if we take the widest and wisest view of Cause," Eliot once wrote apropos of Matthew Arnold, "there is no such thing as a Lost Cause because there is no such thing as a Gained Cause." Both terms are relative — and so too are definitions like Roundhead and Cavalier, or Anglican and Protestant, since political and denominational differences do not last beyond the grave and should not be emphasized where the "Chill /Fingers of yew" curl down on all alike.

The yew is the tree of graveyards, and that is why Eliot refers to the sanctified ground beneath them in the closing line of *The Dry Salvages* as nourishing

> The life of significant soil.

Graveyards are places where (in the next Quartet) all must accept "the constitution of silence" and be "folded in a single party." For if the Little Gidding village with its associations of a beaten king who sheltered there at nightfall and a community that was destroyed

> . . . leave us — a symbol:
> A symbol perfected in death,

then such defeats must always remain inconclusive. Otherwise the death of a martyr, or a hill such as Calvary, would symbolize defeat, not victory. Like the compound ghost who is "one and many," so too this movement's ghosts and the many who supported them are folded by death in "a single party," just as in the *Paradiso* Dante's saints are folded in the petals of "a single snow-white rose." And yet to apprehend fully "the intersection of the timeless moment" remains "an occupation for the saint."

For the ordinary man, "there is only the trying," the "hints and guesses, /Hints followed by guesses" that lead to moments of half-understanding: "the moment in the rose-garden, /The moment in the arbour"; the moment walking beside the "strong brown [river] god," "the moment of the yew-tree," or the moment in the tube when the "underground train . . . stops too long between stations"; the moment when is heard the "Whisper of running streams," the sea's "many voices, /Many gods and many voices," or the moment during which "the light fails /On a winter's afternoon, in a secluded chapel," in Huntingdonshire. How perfectly that word *fails* marks the human condition — especially "the failing / Pride or resentment at failing powers" with oncoming age. How perfectly it underlines the fragmentary nature of man's knowledge and the limitation that surrounds all earthly achievement, except that of the saint.

The word saint, however, needs qualification. If it is reserved only for Christians there is shrinkage of vision, since there were holy men dwelling in Argos and Asia long before Christ was born. In their explorations of the life of the spirit, they fashioned out of negatives — the darkness that is light or the stillness that is dancing — paths of affirmation which were later to be followed by doctors and mystics of the Church (Eliot quotes from three — the author of *The Cloud of Unknowing*, Dame Juliana of Norwich, and St. John of the Cross). The point which divides these mystics of the Christian world from the Ancient is the moment when God became man — the event which redeemed time, lent history a purpose, and gave life a meaning. This is Eliot's "point of intersection of the timeless / With time" — a place suspended, as it were, between two phrases, one from the first Quartet, one from the third, which when united read:

> At the still point of the turning world . . .
> . . . is Incarnation.

It is a line whose fragments so joined chart the complete journey from *Burnt Norton* to *Little Gidding*, showing — whether "on the shores of Asia, or in the Edgware Road" —

> the end of all our exploring
> Will be to arrive where we started
> And know the place for the first time.

31

IV. The Plays

ONE OF THE MAIN THEMES OF ELIOT'S PLAYS IS THE MAKING of a saint and the temptations on the way. In *Murder in the Cathedral,* Archbishop Becket, in following a course that may lead to martyrdom, has to recognize that the greatest treason is

To do the right deed for the wrong reason.

In *The Family Reunion,* Harry Monchensey stands on the brink of a possible martyrdom. Ahead of him lies thirst and deprivation; worship before a stony sanctuary and a primitive altar; and a care over lives of humble people. He has passed through despair to the other side where faith lies. He is walking in the steps of Charles de Foucauld, a French martyr whose "death in the desert" is recalled in the closing lines of *Murder in the Cathedral.*

In *The Cocktail Party* (1949), the first of Eliot's post-war comedies, Celia Coplestone joins a nursing missionary order. Like Harry, her faith issues from despair, and her martyrdom, a particularly violent kind, is described in Act III. Eliot regarded this act as an epilogue, and the reason why he added that her crucifixion had taken place "very near an ant hill," was because he was determined that his audience should have no delusions about the final horror of her end. E. Martin Browne, the producer of all his stage works, has recorded that when *The Family Reunion* was first put on in 1939, it "was received with incomprehension." Even Michael Redgrave, who played Harry, admitted at rehearsals that much of Part II baffled him. So ten years later, when Eliot was working within the conventions of West End drama, he was determined that no detail of Celia Coplestone's death should be omitted in bringing home the abiding truth that her martyr's blood, no less than Becket's in the twelfth century, could still enrich the earth.

The belief that sanctity never departs from such hallowed places — whether a medieval cathedral in England or a missionary outpost in the Pacific — recurs again, but differently, in

32

his last two plays. For those who listen carefully, trees and flowers are used as symbols signifying holy ground in both *The Confidential Clerk* (1954) and *The Elder Statesman* (1959).

In the first, Colby Simpkins is a keen gardener whose activities are restricted to a window-box in his London mews flat. This restriction in turn reflects the restriction placed upon his own life by his pursuit of a career concerned with finance rather than with pursuing his true vocation which is to be a musician. Only when he accepts his role to be an organist in the parish church (it is hinted that he may eventually read for religious orders) does he reach that point where, in inhabiting the garden of the soul, he shall "hear music that no one else [can]" and where "the flowers shall have a scent that [no one else can] smell." Similarly, it is only on the terrace garden of Badgley Court nursing home, that Lord Claverton in *The Elder Statesman* is "brushed by the wing of happiness" and learns for the first time in his dying hour the meaning of that love which (in the *Four Quartets*) costs not less than everything. When he leaves the stage in Act III to die under a beech tree where "it is quiet and cold," some may be reminded of the juniper tree in *Ash-Wednesday* under which the purified bones sang, others of the grove under which Oedipus dies at Colonus.

This interpretation of the five Eliot plays is based on seeing them in production, and naturally every dramatist meets his most important testing time in the "live" theatre. When *The Confidential Clerk* first appeared in print — a few months after its opening at the Edinburgh Festival of 1953 — several critics pounced on Lady Elizabeth Mulhammer's lines:

> He was run over. By a rhinoceros
> In Tanganyika.

They said they were sub-Pinero. Nonetheless in performance they came across extremely well — much more successfully than many passages in the choruses of *Murder in the Cathedral* where the difficulty is to train actors to catch the rhythm of the lines and yet at the same time impersonate the spontaneity of peasant wives and daughters welcoming back to Canterbury their Archbishop in 1170. The best solution, I believe, is to let them speak with a country burr.

Eliot's first experiments with the use of a chorus date back to his "Fragment of the Agon" which he published in 1927. In the year before, he had published his "Fragment of a Prologue," and then in 1932 he joined the two together in a 32-page book under the title of *Sweeney Agonistes*. Already he had issued a number of essays on the drama, contributed a regular theatre column about the contemporary London stage to *The Criterion,* and discussed at considerable length the nature of poetry and drama. Now he was beginning to put his theories into practice.

Sweeney belongs to the world of ex-pugilists in Britain who end up by becoming pub-keepers. At the old English music-hall — of which Eliot had been a loyal devotee — they could be seen night after night joining in the songs and shouting for more. The repertoires that they loved best were a mixture of horror and sentiment: of girls swooning in tropic isles, and of villains drowning them in baths of lysol. Sweeney is true to type. But he is also universal. He stands for every man who has ever had the desire — perhaps only "once in a lifetime" — to "do a girl in." So much for one interpretation. Another, suggested by the epigraph from Orestes is that perhaps Sweeney is an example of the kind of man who instead of plucking out his eye to enter the kingdom of Heaven, decides to pluck out what he has seen. This leads to retribution — or, how else explain the sinister knocking with which the piece ends in the book? (*How reconcile two such opposed readings?* was a question once put to the dramatist by the Oxford producer and don, Nevill Coghill. "Why is either wrong?" came the elusive reply.)

In June 1965, at a special program presented at the London Globe Theatre called "Homage to T. S. Eliot," a last — and as yet unpublished — short scene was added to *Sweeney Agonistes*. This introduced an Old Gentleman who looked like Father Christmas, but said that he was Time. He revealed as well that he waited for "the lost trains that [brought] in the last souls after midnight." The fact that the trains are *lost* and the souls *last,* and not the other way round, should be noted. Theatrically speaking, it is an early example of Eliot's use of mystery to baffle an audience. It is part of his later trade in ghostly tempters, unidentified guests, and "guardians" who either turn out to be the Greek Furies or old women who see more than most and yet, like Julia Shufflethwaite in *The Cocktail Party,* keep mislaying their spectacles.

Eliot followed the fragmentary Sweeney melodramas with two tragedies and three comedies. Tragedy demands a star part. The role of Macbeth must always remain a star part — and so it is with Becket in *Murder in the Cathedral* and Harry in *The Family Reunion.* This is not to say that there cannot be different interpretations of Macbeth, Becket and Harry, but that the plays are dominated by their presence. But in a play like Congreve's *Love for Love,* the star part can either be Valentine, Tattle or Ben. Likewise, although Rex Harrison and Alec Guiness in London and New York made Sir Henry Harcourt-Reilly the star part in *The Cocktail Party* because they were star actors, it would be possible to conceive of productions in which the balance could be shifted to Edward Chamberlayne (his part is longer than Sir Henry's), or to Celia Coplestone. In an interview with Donald Hall of *The Paris Review,* Eliot stated that she was "the most important character in the play."

This difference between tragedy and comedy is worth stressing because it was to comedy that Eliot gave his complete attention after the war. *The Family Reunion,* his only other play set in the twentieth century, was a psychological study, based on the Greek story of Orestes, and in one sense it is partly a re-working of *Sweeney Agonistes,* because Harry, like Sweeney, is tormented with doubts about his desire to do his wife in and the fact that she slipped overboard in mid-Atlantic. But did she slip? What is the link between desire and reality, or event and wish-fulfillment? Only when the truth about his parents' relationship is made clear, is the burden of guilt lifted and the way made clear for him to say:

I must follow the bright angels.

So ends the middle scene of Part II. Harry has discovered who he is, and what he must do. The loop of time has come full cycle. And the journey for Harry, no less than for his creator, has also been one of discovery. It may even have been one of surprise, because the writer of tragedy does not seek, but find. At some point the characters that he has created

35

take over. In contrast, the writer of comedy invents — and consequently the framework has to be much tighter.

What Eliot sought to capture in his last three plays was the tone of post-war London between 1949-59. All three are mainly set in the capital — though the plots in each case spring from Greek themes: the *Alcestis* and the *Ion* of Euripides, and the *Oedipus at Colonus* of Sophocles. They are a mixture of several kinds of comedy: Gilbert and Sullivan, Nöel Coward and "divine comedy." And it is the latter element — something that Eliot invented — which gives them their unique place in the history of drama. For beneath the marvellous speakability of their cocktail chatter and small talk is the question facing each character — *Who am I?* It is Prufrock's voice speaking through them and reaching the conclusion which he never reached — that is, that a man must either choose to be himself, or be nothing. If he is true to his calling as a potter or musician, then he must practice his art; and even if he is not very good at it, as is the case of both tycoon and private secretary in *The Confidential Clerk,* then that does not ultimately matter. Celia Coplestone in *The Cocktail Party* is a woman of passion, but until advised by Sir Henry Harcourt-Reilly, her mistake has been to channel it to men who could not reciprocate it. By letting her come to grips with the potentiality of her passion, Sir Henry is able to direct her to join a nursing order of missionaries, and like a good Jungian psychiatrist he sees that the choice is made by her alone. In *The Elder Statesman,* Lord Claverton has to free himself from the self that pretends to be something that it is not, for it is only by becoming *no one* that he can become *some one.* Only on the point of death does he find out what the true meaning of life is.

In a tragedy these would be sad truths learnt too late; but in a "divine comedy" they are religious paradoxes. Yet these moments can only be fleeting, and they must be interspersed with scenes of mistaken identity and banter about family weaknesses, because echoing through the plays, and stated first in *Murder in the Cathedral* and then repeated in *Burnt Norton,* is the fact that

> human kind
> Cannot bear very much reality.

In the end this is why, self-sufficient as the plays are in themselves, their real interest derives as footnotes to the poems; they are extensions of the Boston of Prufrock, the Antwerp of Gerontion, and the "unreal cities" watched over by Tiresias.

Among these footnotes, as it were, is a sub-footnote. This concerns *The Rock,* a pageant play for which Eliot wrote the scenario in 1934. Its purpose was distinctly propagandist: to raise money on behalf of the Forty-Five Churches Fund of the Diocese of London. It is a work that brings together music-hall songs and political cabaret; historical sketches ranging from Anglo-Saxon days to Mosley's Blackshirts of the 'Thirties; and comments on the Keynsian theory of economics, Dunne's view of time, and Douglas's plan for social credit. There are one or two rather feeble private jokes: "I reckon you're something like a bank clerk."

As a commissioned effort, it was more than adequate, because what distinguished it were the 8 chorus speeches, which, since 1935, have been incorporated in all editions of the *Collected Poems*. But "the book of words" as the author described the script, he let go out of print. It is no great loss. It remains a work more of interest for the historian than literary critic.

V. Criticism

ELIOT WAS NEVER NIGGARDLY IN HIS PRAISE OF THOSE WHO had helped him, beginning with Mr. Roger Conant Hatch, who had been his first English master at Smith Academy. The dedication of *The Waste Land* is one of the most generous in literary history: "For Ezra Pound — *il miglior fabbro* (the better workman)." Another name that should be mentioned in this context is Sir Bruce Richmond, one of the most invisible and yet influential creators of literary taste in this century. For years he kept his name out of *Who's Who* and was only obliged to yield when New College Oxford made him a Doctor of Letters. But when in 1961 he celebrated a quiet 90th birthday, Eliot did not fail to pay his dues to this "great editor" with his hidden "genius," because it was from 1902 to 1936 that Richmond was in control of *The Times Literary Supplement.*

Anonymous literary journalism such as the *TLS* maintains has often come in for severe knocks, but one of its incalculable values is that it teaches writers that what may be permissible when signed, can become tasteless eccentricity when unsigned. Occasionally spite or obtuse blindness may creep in — and the *TLS* review of *Prufrock & Other Observations* was an example of the latter. "Inarticulate" and "uninspired" were two of the verdicts passed, and "will hardly be read by many with enjoyment" was the general tenor of the notice. But for the most part Eliot thought that the merits of anonymous reviewing far outweighed the few lapses, because, as he declared in his birthday tribute to Richmond, such journalism instructed a critic how "to moderate his dislikes and crotchets", and how "to write in a temperate and partial way."

The province assigned by Richmond to Eliot was Elizabethan and Jacobean poetry and drama, but as Richmond became surer of his new reviewer, so he allowed him to make excursions outside of the original area. "A chance remark in conversation revealed that I was an ardent admirer of Bishop Lancelot Andrewes, and I was at once commissioned to write the leader which appears among my collected papers." Books as often as not were used as "pegs" for review-articles, and from 1919 onwards Eliot wrote a good many for the *TLS* during the next sixteen years. But before he had met Richmond, several had been published by Middleton Murry in *The Atheneum.* One of these was "pegged" to J. M. Robertson's study of *The Problem of Hamlet,* and it was in the course of this review-article, which came out on September 26th, 1919 — his 31st birthday — that Eliot launched the term "objective correlative." Here is the passage:

> The only way of expressing emotion in the form of art is by finding an "objective correlative"; in other words, a set of objects, a chain of events which shall be the formula of that *particular* emotion; such that when the external facts, which must terminate in sensory experience, are given, the emotion is immediately evoked.

Since this was first written, much debate has ensued round the exact meaning of the term — a fair degree of it being intellectual showing off. It is worth noting that when W. H. Auden came to broadcast his Eliot obituary on January 4th, 1965, he admitted that he "would be hard put to it to say exactly what the objective correlative [was]." But in admitting this, he put his finger on Eliot's significance as a critic when in the next breath he recalled his "extraordinary gift for surprising quotations." "His quotation of six lines from Dryden," he went on, "suddenly made me see the poet in a new light." The lines (Mr. Auden tells me) were these, and come from Dryden's *Secular Masque* of 1700:

> All, all of a piece throughout!
> Thy Chase had a Beast in View;
> Thy Wars brought nothing about;
> Thy Lovers were all untrue.
> 'Tis well an Old Age is out,
> And time to begin a New.

Eliot first quoted these lines in his *TLS* review-article of Mark van Doren's *John Dryden,* which came out in 1921. In passing, he paused to remark that whereas these very fine lines were not included in the *Oxford Book of English Verse,* there were included some very indifferent extracts from Shelley. Revaluations always take time to have an effect, and in 1941 *The Concise Cambridge History of English Literature* still referred to the *Secular Masque* as a theatrical piece of "no enduring value." In university circles, the recognition of Eliot's criticism has been chiefly a post-war development.

His talent for choosing rewarding quotations, and then illuminating them, is well demonstrated in his critical essay on Ben Jonson, where he quotes this line from *Poetaster* (1602):

> Light, I salute thee, but with wounded nerves . . .

He comments: "Men may not talk in that way, but the Spirit of Envy does, and in the words of Jonson envy is a real and living person. It is not human life that informs envy . . . but it is energy of which human life is only another variety."

At their best, many of Eliot's critical articles are anthologies in miniature. Yet numerous as these essays are, they are not quite as all-embracing as some have supposed. There is nothing on Jules Laforgue, of whom he said: "I owe more to [him] than to any one poet." And the reason why there is nothing is that the needed commission to write such a piece was not forthcoming. In the early days, the need for money allowed him to write only commissioned pieces, which meant that nearly all his criticism took the form either of anniversary or review-articles. His piece on Lancelot Andrewes in 1926 marked the third centenary since the death of that Anglican divine.

The essays that were not written under financial pressure were either lectures such as the Charles Eliot Norton Lectures delivered at Harvard between 1932-33 (and subsequently issued under the title of *The Use of Poetry and the Use of Criticism*), or papers written for public occasions such as "The Three Voices of Poetry" which he delivered in 1953 at the eleventh annual lecture of the National Book League in London. As Eliot grew older and more famous, these demands to give papers became more frequent. Nor did he complain, since he saw the inconvenient obligation of sitting upon committees, who, later, would press him to give papers, as part of the tradition of public service — a tradition which both his father and grandfather had firmly impressed upon their families.

The presence of an audience — whether of students or the public — tends to force upon a writer the need to clarify his ideas; and sometimes his writing may be all the better for having been intended to be spoken aloud. (I doubt if any audience could take in at one sitting the idea behind the "objective correlative.") Certainly, once in his sixties, Eliot's humorous asides at public occasions increased: "H. L. Mencken . . . whose monumental book on the American language is a philologist's picnic." That comes from an address given at Washington University in the 1950s.

If there was a gain of informality in the lectures and papers of Eliot's last decade, there was also a loss: too often a mild chit-chat took the place of that extinction of personality which at the outset of his career he had insisted was necessary if the artist was to progress; and by artist he meant the critic no less than the poet, since both drew on the same kind of sensibility, but employed it differently to present their interpretation. He saw no reason why a critic should not be as inspired as a poet, and sometimes the two callings fused. He would point to Samuel Johnson and Coleridge. He could have pointed to himself, since his review-articles were every bit as much voyages of discovery as his poems. That is why so much of his criticism up to his middle fifties can be read as a direct commentary on the work that he himself was writing. A remark of his made when he was 42 about Baudelaire's attitude to sin illustrates this. "So far as we do evil or good," he writes in the Preface to Christopher Isherwood's translation of the *Journaux Intimes,* "we are human; and it is better, in a paradoxical way, to do evil than to do nothing; at least, we exist." Four years later, in 1934, the same Baudelairean argument is to be found expressed in Eliot's primer of modern heresy called *After Strange Gods.*

After the publication of the *Four Quartets,* he wrote less than half a dozen poems. His tribute in 1948 to Walter de la Mare on the occasion of his 75th birthday, and his eleven-line dedication to his wife in 1959 at the beginning of the printed version of *The Elder Statesman,* are moving and highly personal: but they are best summed up in his own words as "Occasional Verses." "The Cultivation of Christmas Trees" was the only real poem that he wrote, and this, in comparison with the other four in the *Ariel* series, appears to be somewhat forced. The truth is that his poetry springs were running dry, and as this was happening, so the quality of his prose was being drained of its earlier distinction. Good things still came, but they came more rarely. Yet his last essay on George Herbert did still demonstrate John Crowe Ransom's observation of a quarter of a century before that "no critic proceeds so regularly by the technique of comparative quotation."

In George Herbert, Eliot noted that "feeling seemed to control thought," whereas in Donne "thought seemed to control feeling." The difference, he argued, could be illustrated by the closing couplet of two of their sonnets: Donne's

for I
Except you'enthrall mee, never shall be free,
Nor ever chast, except, you ravish mee,

and Herbert's:

Church-bels beyond the starres heard, the souls bloud,
The land of spices; something understood.

The first was, "in the best sense, *wit";* and the second, "the kind of poetry which . . . may be called *magical."*

His last book, *To Criticize the Critic,* was issued posthumously, and is for the most part a gathering together of papers that attempt to nullify much of what he had written earlier. "I have lost interest . . ." is the tone; "If asked whether I still hold the same view, I can only say 'I don't care' or 'I don't know.' " The collection makes for sad reading — the tragedy of age, like the comment Pound was overheard to make about his own earlier work just after attending the Eliot Memorial Service at Westminster Abbey: "It doesn't mean a damn thing, a damn thing."

In the 1940s, Eliot gave the call that "old men should be explorers." But this was not always to be so in his own case after he was 55. The title-essay of his last book is proof of that. This, however, would be a niggardly note on which to close a section on a critic who at his finest had no rival. So one final quotation — a definition of wit that comes from the essay that he contributed to the *TLS* on Andrew Marvell when he was 33, at the height of his powers, and that helps also to illuminate many of the lines which he singled out in the essay he wrote on George Herbert when he was 74.

> Wit is not erudition; it is sometimes stifled by erudition . . . . It is not cynicism, though it has a kind of toughness which may be confused with cynicism by the tender-minded. It is confused with erudition because it belongs to an educated mind, rich in generations of experience, and it is confused with cynicism because it implies a constant inspection and criticism of experience. It involves, probably, a recognition, implicit in the expression of every experience, of other kinds of experience which are possible.

VI. Conclusion

ELIOT LEFT IT IN HIS WILL THAT THERE WAS TO BE NO Official Biography. Nor has all his work yet appeared, or been kept in print. Some of his essays on the later Shakespearean plays that he showed to Robert Speaight in manuscript, have never been issued. In 1949 a thousand copies of *The Undergraduate Poems* that he published while at college in *The Harvard Advocate* were reprinted: but as they had been printed without authorization, most of the edition was withdrawn. All

42

that is promised by his publishers for the future, is a selection of his Letters and a reissue of his *Poems Written in Early Youth* that first came out in 1950 in a privately printed edition of 12 copies.

So, those who want an authorized Life, and who like their poets' lives tied up in neat parcels, will be disappointed. They will have to make do with passing references, culled from the writings of other men. John Betjeman, with whom Eliot was once a schoolmaster on the same staff, has written of the poet's delight at living at a London address called Bina Gardens. Robert Giroux, his American publisher, has recorded how when he asked him if he agreed with the definition that editors were failed writers, Eliot had replied: "Perhaps, but so are most writers." Lord Moran in his diaries has described the post-war meeting between Churchill and Eliot and how, when the poet's name was mentioned, it left only a blank on the elder statesman's face.

In drawing a portrait, then, the method has to be one of following hints — "hints followed by guesses." And this is precisely what Eliot would have liked, because it is a method in which surprises will frequently recur. Churchmen who admired the serious intent behind his *Idea of a Christian Society* (1939) and educationalists who praised his *Notes Towards the Definition of Culture* (1949) may find themselves in for a series of shocks when they learn of his love of whoopee cushions and joke cigars. But no man can always stay at the sublime heights, and if paradoxically enough some of the more conservative elements in his family were baffled by the sublime heights that he reached in his work, then at least they would have understood his practical joker side. In St. Louis, the Eliots loved April 1st — although the fooling that they pursued was never intended to hurt; the surprises were nice ones — like discovering an unexpected gift.

Nor did fame put the slightest break on Eliot's love of jokes as both a man and writer. When he mentioned the island of Kinkanja in *The Cocktail Party,* researchers beatled off trying to trace it: but it proved imaginary — like the island of Tanzatatapoo with which he had fooled his English master in a short story that he wrote when he was 16. After the war, having addressed a vast audience in Minneapolis that had gathered in the sports stadium, he was asked what it felt like to speak to 14,000 people. "Not 14,000," he replied, "but 13,523." The precision was typical — a reminder of his "Triumphal March" with its procession beginning with 5,800,000 rifles and carbines, and ending with 1,150 field bakeries. This list, by the way, had been borrowed from "the list of things surrendered or destroyed by the Germans after Versailles" and then been incorporated in the poem.

Much has been made of this and other borrowings: the fact that "Christ the tiger" was a phrase first used by Bishop Lancelot Andrewes, or that certain lines from Sherlock Holmes's story "The Musgrave Ritual" are repeated by the second Tempter in *Murder in the Cathedral*. Yet there is a world of difference between borrowing and copying, for whereas copying leads to pastiche, borrowing can bring an old text to life in a new context; tradition is recast by the individual talent. For no artist can stand without the support of his creative ancestors, nor suppress the resurgence of ancient themes and race memories. In releasing and controling these vital forces, Eliot relied on a conscious use of synthesis and an acceptance of synchronizations that took place at a subconscious level. It may be explained thus.

In the subconscious mind, both church and brothel stand with their doors open. Out of each, images stream upward into the conscious mind. They arrive there in no set order, nor in even numbers, nor at the same time. Stream-of-conscious writing is a twentieth-century term — and it sums up exactly what some modern writers do with the raw material of their art. Eliot was always interested in the term, but what he attempted to do in his own work was to synthesize the images from both streams by means of a contrapuntal technique which would both balance and contrast the sordid with the spiritual, the matter-of-fact with the fanciful. It was a method that allowed him to telescope time, so that in *The Waste Land* the one-eyed merchant can be said to equal the Phoenician sailor who equals Ferdinand Prince of Naples; he is three characters in one. It allowed him also in a poem like "Sweeney Erect" to employ a marvellous shorthand by which the bath in which Sweeney luxuriates can be linked with Christ's baptism in the Jordan. The long short story is a comparatively

44

new art-form, but such were Eliot's powers of concentrating his vision that it might be said he pioneered the way for the long short poem — a new art-form that is now on the increase.

And it is perhaps right that the final accent of this essay should fall on what he pioneered, as well as on what he prophecied; on the long fight that he had with trying to "use words, and every attempt . . . a wholly new start." Memoirs with their pictures of the poet drinking Russion stout or sporting an eyeglass have their place; so too have the research articles that have penetrated his many disguises, beginning with Mr. Conybeare. The danger is that if such idiosyncrasies and eccentricities are blown up too much, essentials can become lost in inessentials. Literary perspective goes by the board, and the poetry becomes swamped by trivia. In resisting this temptation there remains the paradox that perspective itself is always changing, because not only do past works of art assert themselves in new ones, but each new work of art illuminates all the works of art that preceded it.

Life is lived forwards but interpreted backwards, and every completed poem for the author of the *Four Quarters* comes to represent either a full-stop or a milestone between "here," "now," and "always." What a contrast this offers to Prufrock measuring out his afternoons with coffee spoons. And yet it is precisely by these subtle contrasts and variations that Eliot not only gives a structural whole to his poetry, but a coherence and consistency to all his writing — whether prose or poetry. "I shall say it again" is a phrase that recurs in both. Or, as he put it at the beginning of his career as a reviewer: "I merely criticize poetry in order to create it." Moreover, it was just after his undergraduate days had ended that he became aware "for the first time that a man who is capable of experience finds himself in a different world in every decade of his life; he sees it with different eyes, and the material for his art is [thus] constantly renewed." Similarly, for readers of each fresh decade or generation, new meanings will come to light in a poet's work.

To those of Eliot's own generation and the one following it, his immediate achievements were twofold: to take English poetry out of its Georgian backwater into the midstream of European poetry, and to re-create an interest in Dante, the

45

Jacobeans, John Donne and the Metaphysicals, John Dryden, and the French Symbolists.

His success was also twofold: as a critic his work was very soon saluted by F. R. Leavis at Downing College Cambridge and by F. O. Matthiessen at Harvard, and as a poet and publisher he became, and remained for forty years, the dominating figure on the Transatlantic scene. In 1948, Kathleen Raine wrote: "Few young poets . . . have not at some time . . . registered a parcel of poems to Faber. . . ." She continued: "Hints dropped in a line of his verse . . . sent us off to discover what Krishna meant, or what St. John of the Cross envisaged by the Dark Night, or why an allusion from Mallarmé stirred overtones so nostalgic." Hers is a judgment that has been so generally seconded by her contemporaries that it has now become a part of accepted literary history.

But it is Eliot the prophet rather than Eliot the pioneer who is the figure who may well come to dominate the remainder of this century. Since the end of the second Vatican Council in 1965, it has become increasingly clear that the structures of society and religion which prevailed in the ancient world and in Europe are no longer valid. In *The Waste Land* Tiresias foresees this, but foresees it in terms of a world trying to subsist on a civilized but non-Christian mentality. (The poet's own standpoint then was Buddhist.) Likewise, just as it is becoming increasingly clear that the old structures of religion must be replaced by new ones, so also the increase in speed and travel is making imperative the need for more communication between the different religions. Structures will have to be found that are universal enough to accommodate the concept of "one world." In fact it would be true to say of the *Four Quartets* that a non-Christian mystic could be as much at home in them as a Christian mystic — and it was this precise point that was made in 1945 in the book columns of Middleton Murry's little review, *The Adelphi*. It was suggested there that, compared with *Murder in the Cathedral,* the Quartets exhibited "greater depth, greater intensity, and greater beauty. . . . , but less Christianity." "Is it possible," the reviewer went on, "that the level reached . . . is beyond Christianity?"

In retrospect, this appears a characteristic post-Hiroshima comment, because in those days, when the Bomb had cast its first terrifying shadow, the spirit of universality that was to be introduced later by Pope John seemed a hope beyond the wildest dreams of men. In 1945 Eliot's was a lone voice crying in the desert, and the Christianity of his later plays like *The Cocktail Party* struck many as being singularly wide-embracing and tolerant. Indeed, today's perspective would not suggest that the Quartets and later plays were reaching to a level beyond Christianity, but rather that Christianity is now reaching out to a level that could never have been sought while the old structures held.

It therefore seems worth putting on the record the little-known statement made by Eliot in 1963 when he received the Campion Award from the Catholic Book Club in New York: "The gladness with which the Christian Churches of every description recognized the activities for ecumenicity of your great Pope John testifies to a universal longing for unity." Four years previously, Pope John had sent him a letter commending his services to religion.

A poet's best biography is his work, and Eliot was probably wise to block an official one, because in a writer's life

Every phrase and every sentence is an end and a beginning,
Every poem an epitaph.

So now when it comes to writing his own epitaph, perhaps the inscription in East Coker Church, where his ashes lie, adds all that needs to be said:

Pray for the repose of the soul of T. S. Eliot, poet